BEGINNING
SIGN
LANGUAGE
SERIES

Songs in Sign

by S. Harold Collins

Illustrated by Kathy Kifer, and Dahna Solar

Songs in Sign presents familiar songs fully illustrated in Signed English. These are songs that will encourage beginning signers And develop their facility for signing.

Music and signs are presented for six songs:

Special thanks to: Jeff Corbett, Amanda Corbett, Arias Solar, Elena Collins, Emily Collins, Carissa Albin, Colleen Kerns, Austin Griff   ith, Ariel Solar, Paul Albin.

www.garlicpress.com

If You're Happy

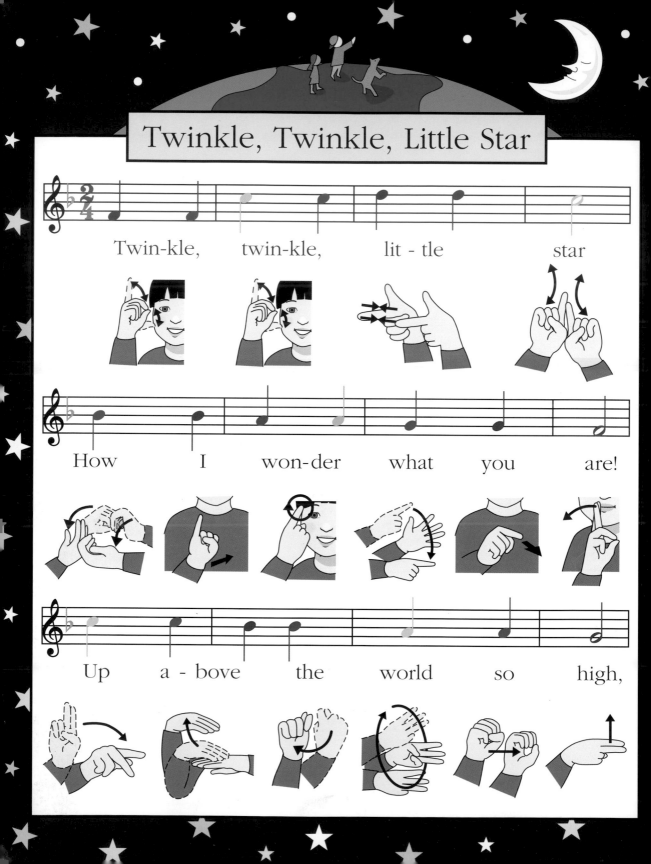

Bingo

Row, Row, Row Your Boat

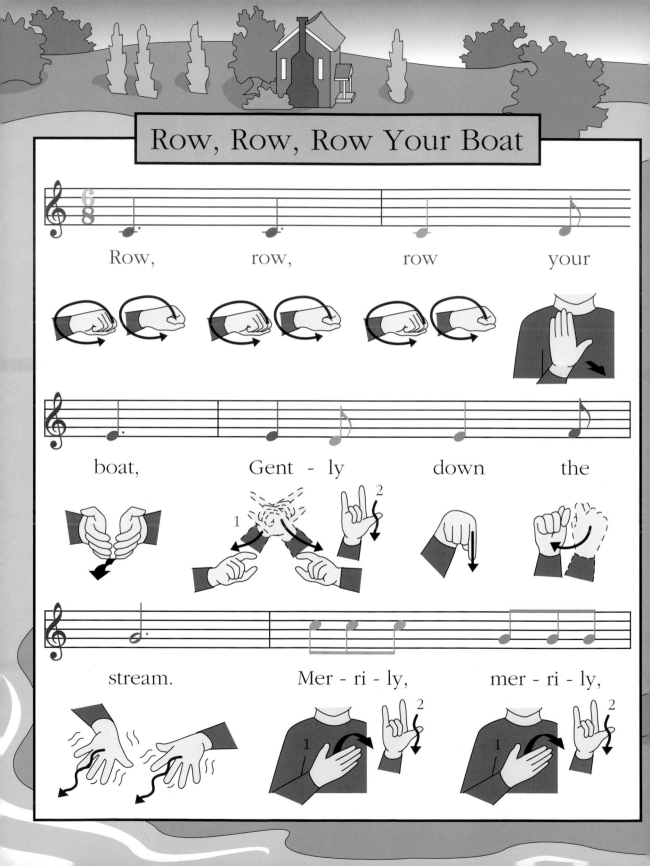

The Muffin Man

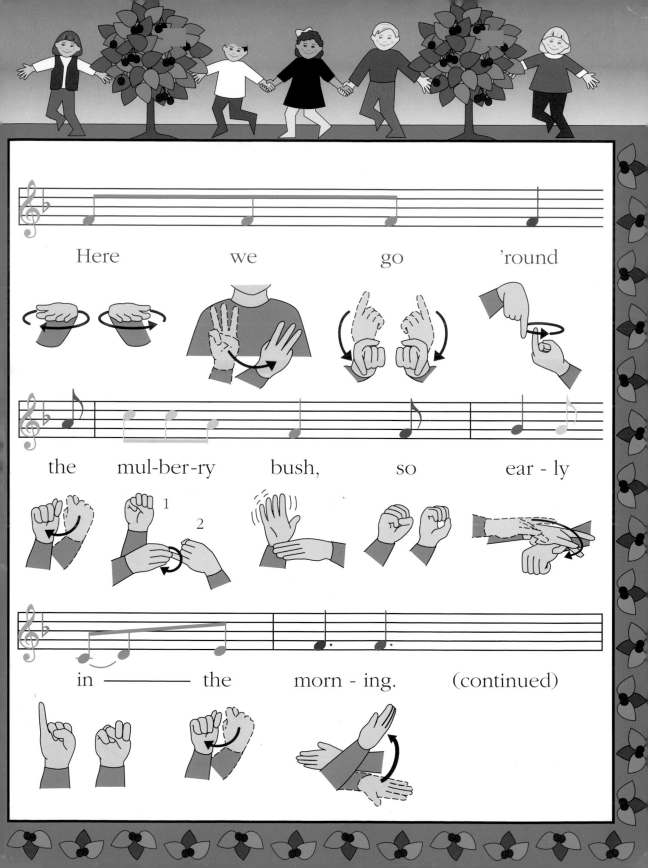